# PRAY LIKE A SAINT

## 10 ancient prayer principles

James Fox Robinson

ISBN 978-0-9559781-2-8

anewloom publishing

www.jamesfoxrobinson.online

Typeset in FoglihtenNo07, Calibri, Book Antiqua

" there is a fabric of the old way of
being society and being church.

we are not about patching the fabric of
that old garment but seeking to set up

# ANEWLOOM

to weave the new fabric for
tomorrows society of the kingdom "

# Cont

# ents

Do not forget that the value and interest of life is not so much to do conspicuous things ... as to do ordinary things with the perception of their enormous value.

- *Teilhard de Chardin*

# Preface

I began engaging with creative prayer as a teenager when the 24-7 prayer movement started. As a creative, visual minded person, I had always struggled with the word-centric prayers I encountered in church and I was excited that other people were exploring visual and kinaesthetic forms of prayer.

While working at a conference and retreat centre, I encountered a daily rhythm of prayer - morning, midday and compline. Being on the rota to deliver prayers, I was able to experiment with different styles, using theatre, film and atmosphere to create reflective environments.

As the Prayer and Spirituality Enabler for a Diocese of the Church of England, I had the privilege of exploring a broad range of prayers and types of prayer. Some of the material included here, I first discovered while creating resources for a spiritual direction course.

I also began to engage with ancient monastic forms of prayer and joined the Third Order Franciscans. Around this time I was also exploring the biblical and religious history of creativity within spirituality.

The material here is just a taste, not an in depth look or academic study of prayer. It is an introduction to a few concepts which I have found personally useful in my journey to engage with the divine.

If you've never experienced prayer beyond Sunday intercessions, if you are interested in monastic rhythm or you're looking for inspiration for different ways to engage in prayer - I hope the ideas curated here will be of use.

I do not believe there are hard and fast rules for prayer and I have purposefully not tried to define it here. I encourage you to let go of whatever definitions of prayer you may have and engage with this material as an explorer - if you find you don't get on with something, move on, if something intrigues you , rest with it for a while.

**James Fox Robinson**

"It's one of my theories that when people give you advice, they're really just talking to themselves in the past"

- Austin Kleon

This book contains what I needed to read when I was young. These are prayer practices which I've had to stumble upon,  grapple with, explore and find a rhythm for in my own life.

These are practices that anyone can engage with.

In other words - this book is for you.

Let's Begin

① 1

# Contemplation

# Teresa

## of Avila

Teresa of Ávila lived in the 16th Century. She was a Spanish noblewoman who became a nun. She joined a monastic order called the Carmelites. Teresa helped to change the church through writing and sharing ideas on contemplative prayer. She became a saint more than 400 years after her death. The church celebrates her life on October 15th.

# be a
# spectator

> "Prayer is an act of love; words are not needed. Even if sickness distracts from thoughts, all that is needed is the will to love."
>
> *- Saint Teresa of Avila*

Until the 6th Century, mysticism was known as contemplatio, the Latin word from which we get our 'contemplation'. There is something still intrinsically mystical about Christian contemplation today, it's about the wonder, the mystery, the awe of the divine.

But other root words for contemplation mean 'being a spectator' who considers, speculates, looks at...

> "contemplation and mysticism speak
> of the eye of love which is looking at,
> gazing at, aware of divine realities."
>
> *- William Johnson*

The word Contemplation is used to mean a variety of things in today's world and can encompass a number of the other practices shared in this book. However, St Teresa of Avila in *The Way of Perfection* explains that contemplative prayer is 'a Divine union, in which the Lord takes His delight in the soul and the soul takes its delight in Him.' This alludes to contemplation as a great act of love - we desire God and God desires us.

"Prayer in my opinion is nothing else than an intimate sharing between friends; it means taking time frequently to be alone with Him who we know loves us. The important thing is not to think much but to love much and so do that which best stirs you to love. Love is not great delight but desire to please God in everything."

*- Saint Teresa of Avila*

"Gregory the Great (sixth century), summarizing the Christian contemplative tradition, expressed it as 'resting in God.' This was the classical meaning of Contemplative Prayer in the Christian tradition for the first sixteen centuries."

*- Thomas Keating*

"Contemplative prayer removes us from the driver's seat."

*- Ed Cyzewski*

An exercise long used among Christians for acquiring contemplation is that of focusing the mind by constant repetition on a phrase or word, a 'saying'.

Saint John Cassian recommended use of the phrase 'O God, make speed to save me: O Lord, make haste to help me'

Another formula for repetition is the Jesus Prayer, which has been called 'the mantra of the Orthodox Church'.

# Lord Jesus Christ,
# Son of God,
# have mercy on me,
# a sinner.

The author of *The Cloud of Unknowing* recommended use of a monosyllabic word, such as 'God' or 'Love'. Early Christians used the watchword 'Maranatha' which means 'Come Lord!'.

# Sayings

Peace I leave with you, my
peace I give unto you
*John 14. 27*

Launch out into the deep
*Luke 5. 4*

Be glad and rejoice for ever
in that which I create
*Isaiah 65. 18*

Be still, and know that
I am God
*Psalm 46. 10*

# a suggested model

Contemplative prayer can be as short as 5 minutes or as long as you wish. It may help to place a picture of Jesus in front of you, or just choose a quiet space. You may choose to have instrumental music.

1. Settle into a comfortable position, taking slow, deep breaths to help quiet yourself.

2. Focus your attention on the image of Jesus or your chosen saying.

3. Acknowledge the things that are trying to get your attention; thoughts, worries, plans, aches and pains, sights and sounds around you. Slowly let these things go. If you feel distracted during this prayer, just quietly bring yourself back to your reflection.

4. In your silence and stillness, let God's Spirit within you make itself known.

5. Do not expect anything to 'happen', put yourself in God's hands.

# Mystery

"Contemplative prayer is the simple expression of the mystery of prayer. It is a gaze of faith fixed on Jesus, an attentiveness to the Word of God, a silent love. It achieves real union with the prayer of Christ to the extent that it makes us share in his mystery"

*- from the Catechism of the Catholic Church*

"All difficulties in prayer can be traced to one cause: praying as if God were absent."

*- Teresa of Avila*

2

# The Exa men

# Ignatius
## of Loyola

Ignatius of Loyola lived 1491 – 1556. He was a Spanish
priest and theologian who co-founded the religious
order called the Society of Jesus (Jesuits). The Jesuit order
served the Pope as missionaries, and they were bound by a
vow of special obedience. He recorded his methods for
praying, as a simple set of meditations, prayers, and
other mental exercises called 'the spiritual exercise' which
were first published in 1548. Ignatius became a saint in 1622
and the church celebrate his life on 31st July.

"But what is so utterly foreign to many is the experience of falling in love with God. Religion, for them, is an intellectual exercise rooted in the individual conscience, rather than a response to a God who holds out a hand to say, Let's have an adventure!"

- *Timothy M. Gallagher*

St. Ignatius of Loyola included in his Spiritual Exercises a prayer called 'the Examen'. The Daily Examen is a technique of prayerful reflection on the events of the day in order to detect God's presence and discern his direction for us.

James Martin suggests we think of it as a movie playing in your head.

"Push the play button and run through your day, from start to finish, from your rising in the morning to preparing to go to bed at night. Notice what made you happy, what made you stressed, what confused you, what helped you be more loving. Recall everything: sights, sounds, feelings, tastes, textures, conversations. Thoughts, words, and deeds, as Ignatius says. Each moment offers a window to where God has been in your day."

St. Ignatius was emphatic about the Examen. He told the early Jesuits that if they for some reason did no other spiritual exercises, they should do this one.

There are many ways to pray the Examen but its basic form is a 5 step process.

1. Place yourself in God's presence

Give thanks for God's great love for you.

2. Pray for  grace

Give space to understand how God is acting in your life.

3. Review your day

Recall specific moments and your feelings at the time.

4. Reflect on what you did, said, or thought

Were you drawing closer to God, or further away?

5. Look toward tomorrow

Think of how you might collaborate more effectively with God's plan. Be specific

The Examen should help you to discover which of your feelings and moods are leading you to God and which are leading you away. As you become used to this prayer process you will begin to notice that your reflections are less about feelings on the surface, and more about movements deep in your heart.

The deeper you are willing to go, the more opportunity The Spirit has to speak. It is at this deeper level of lasting feelings that we truly find ourselves and our real relationship with God. We see what has to be faced, understood, decided and acted upon.

And remember - no experience is too trivial for spiritual investigation.

" The mundane and the humdrum parts of our lives give depth and texture to our relationships with God. Washing the windows and cooking dinner are as much a part of the relationship as graduation day. If it's part of our human experience, God is in it."

- Jim Manney

# some questions to ask...

How was I drawn to God today

a friend, an event, a book, the beauty of nature?

Have I learnt anything about God and His ways

in ordinary occasions, spare moments?

Did I meet Him in

fears, joys, work, misunderstandings, weariness?

Did His Word come alive in

prayer, scriptures, liturgy?

Did I go out to

the lonely, the sorrowful, the discouraged, the needy?

If you're a kinaesthetic person who likes to have something to hold when you pray, this is a simple prayer practice based on the Examen that you can take anywhere.

You need a smooth stone, a rough stone and a precious stone (and maybe a bag to put them in).

Hold the smooth stone and recall the ordinary, normal, humdrum things from your day.

Hold the rough stone and recall the things that made you anxious, fearful or were difficult.

Hold the precious stone and recall something special from the day.

Then ask God what you learnt from those situations and thank God for all of them.

3

# Lectio Divina

# Benedict
## of Nursia

Benedict of Nursia lived 480 to around 543. Benedict founded twelve communities for monks in Italy. His main achievement, the 'Rule of Saint Benedict', contains a set of instructions for his monks to follow. His Rule became one of the most influential religious rules in Christian history. Benedict is the Patron Saint of Europe. He has been called 'the founder of Western Christian monasticism'. The church celebrate his life on July 7th.

The monastic practice of *Lectio Divina* was first established in the 6th century by Benedict of Nursia and was then formalised as a four-step process by the Carthusian monk Guigo II during the 12th century. In the 20th century, the constitution *Dei verbum* of the Second Vatican Council recommended *Lectio Divina* to the general public and its importance was affirmed by Pope Benedict XVI at the start of the 21st century.

## The Four Step Process

1. Lectio (reading)

2. Meditatio (meditating)

3. Oratio (prayer)

4. Contemplatio (contemplation)

"Whatever good work you begin to do, beg of God with most earnest prayer to perfect it."

— *Saint Benedict*

Read
Reflect
Respond
Rest

Lectio Divina is a meditative prayer that can be done alone or as part of a group. It is a prayer, allowing God to speak through the Bible (the living Word). It has been described as a way to "feast on God's Word", so we can use that analogy as we walk through the four steps of this prayer.

## TAKE A BITE
read a brief passage of Scripture

## CHEW
reflect on the phrase that caught your heart

## SAVOUR
respond to what God called to your attention

## DIGEST
rest in God, contemplating the divine words

"Almighty God, give me wisdom to perceive You, intelligence to understand You, diligence to seek You, patience to wait for You, eyes to behold You, a heart to meditate upon You and life to proclaim You, through the power of the Spirit of our Lord Jesus Christ. Amen."

— Benedict of Nursia

Clare of Assisi had a slightly different method which focused on an object or a piece of art rather than the scriptures. We might call it 'Visio Divina'.

## Intueri - gaze

Rest your eyes on what you see, and let it still you. Though eyes and thoughts may be drawn elsewhere, bring them back to the image that is the focus of your prayer.

## Considerare - consider

Involve your mind and your imagination. What is before you? What strikes you in what you see? What do you glimpse of God through it? Do you sense a challenge or a call? Can you give what you are feeling a name?

## Contemplari - contemplate

A mystical seeing, a prayer of silence, of emptying oneself of all but the Spirit of the divine. Rather than being active in your observation or trying to identify new insights, be present to what you have already thought or felt.

## Imitare - imitate

Praying with art, as with all prayer, moves us toward transformation. We become the one we love.

"For the ancients, to meditate is to read a text and to learn it 'by heart' in the fullest sense of this expression, that is, with one's whole being: with the body, since the mouth pronounced it, with the memory which fixes it, with the intelligence which understands its meaning, and with the will which desires to put it into practice."

— **Jean Leclercq**

they are ever ...

blessed are those who ...
who have set their ...

As they pass through ...
the autumn rains ...
make it a place of ...
pools ...

They go from strength ...
till each appears before ...

Hear my prayer, O God ...
Almighty;
listen to me, O God ...
Look upon our shield ...
look with favor on ...
one ...

better is one day in your ...
than a thousand ...
I would rather be a door ...
house of my God
than dwell in the tents ...
wicked.

silence

# John
## the Silent

Saint John the Silent (c. January 8, 454 – c. 558) was a Christian saint known for living alone for seventy-six years. He was given the surname because he loved recollection and silence. John was born in Nicopolis, Armenia. He came from a family of mainly generals and governors. His parents died when he was 18 and he built a monastery where he stayed with 10 young monks. Under John's direction, they led a life of hard work and devotion. John built a reputation for leadership and sanctity, which led the archbishop of Sebaste to consecrate him bishop of Colonia in Armenia. He was only 28 at the time and had no desire for such a role. Nevertheless, he held the post of bishop for nine years before seeking to return to a life of seclusion. Uncertain of his future vocation, he went to Jerusalem. At 38 years old he joined the monastery at St. Sabas, which held 150 monks. After some tests, St. Sabas let John have a separate hermitage for uninterrupted contemplation. For five days a week he fasted and never left his cell. At one point, John stayed in his cell for four years, speaking to no one except the person who brought him necessities.

"Silence is God's first language; everything else is a poor translation."

Thomas Keating

St. John the Silent was a man of few words. He spent the majority of his life in solitude, speaking only when necessary. Many wondered why he chose such a lifestyle, but for St. John, it was a pathway to a deeper connection with God.

As a young man, St. John was known for his eloquence and his love for words. He spoke with ease and was well-versed in the scriptures. However, he began to realise that his words were sometimes empty and lacked the depth he longed for in his relationship with God. He yearned for a deeper connection with the divine, a connection that could not be found in the noise and distractions of the world.

And so, St. John made the decision to enter into a life of silence. He spent long hours in prayer and meditation, seeking to deepen his spiritual connection to God. He found that the practice of silence allowed him to quiet his mind and listen more closely to the still, small voice of God.

# Silence

**Silence is about attention, focus**

Silence can be difficult. Silence can be confusing.
But - entering into it can bring profound transformation.

Entering into silent prayer takes work. It takes discipline and courage to cut through all the little things that distract our minds and hearts to arrive at a sacred and productive moment.

44

"If you still your mind, you can hear your own heart. And at the core of your heart is the indwelling of God."

*- Sister Sylvia Rosell*

In the first book of Kings, we find the story of Elijah encountering God:

He said, 'Go out and stand on the mountain before the Lord, for the Lord is about to pass by.' Now there was a great wind, so strong that it was splitting mountains and breaking rocks in pieces before the Lord, but the Lord was not in the wind; and after the wind an earthquake, but the Lord was not in the earthquake; and after the earthquake a fire, but the Lord was not in the fire; and after the fire a sound of sheer silence. When Elijah heard it, he wrapped his face in his mantle and went out and stood at the entrance of the cave. Then there came a voice to him that said, 'What are you doing here, Elijah?'

*1 Kings 19:11-13*

Elijah is described here as 'hearing' the silence of God.

After the sixth hour, however, when they have risen from table, let them rest in their beds in complete silence; or if, perhaps, anyone desireth to read for himself, let him so read that he doth not disturb others.

The Holy Rule of St. Benedict, Chapter XLVIII

5

# Music

# Augustine
## of Hippo

Augustine of Hippo (13 November 354 – 28 August 430) was a Catholic bishop and theologian, Roman African, doctor of the Church, and Neoplatonic philosopher from Numidia whose writings influenced the development of the Western Church and Western philosophy, and indirectly all of Western Christianity.

Augustine was concerned with the philosophical and mathematical principles integral to enjoying music. His belief, as was common during the time, was that music affected the soul and, thus, could influence and determine the ethics, actions and morals of humans.

# " to sing is to pray twice

Augustine of Hippo

"

St. Augustine of Hippo had a deep and complex relationship with music. Throughout his life, he saw music as a powerful tool for both personal and communal prayer. He believed that music had the ability to elevate the soul and draw it closer to God.

Augustine understood music to be a reflection of the divine harmony found in creation itself. He believed that through music, one could connect with the spiritual realm and enter into a deeper state of prayer. He often spoke of the beauty and power of hymns and chants, and how they could inspire the heart and mind to contemplate the mysteries of faith.

For Augustine, music was not simply a form of entertainment or diversion. Rather, it was a vital part of the spiritual life, a way of expressing and nurturing one's relationship with God. Through music, Augustine found a means of expressing the deepest longings of his soul, and of connecting with the divine presence that lay at the heart of his faith.

"Rhythm and harmony
find their way into the
inward places of the soul."

- Plato

Music
can be a powerful
medium for prayer. When we listen to
or create music, we engage with our emotions
and connect with something beyond ourselves.
This makes music an ideal tool for prayer - it allows
us to express our deepest feelings and connect with
a higher power. In fact, many religious traditions
incorporate music into their prayer practices, from
Gregorian chants to gospel hymns. Whether we are
singing in a choir or simply listening to our favourite
song, music has the ability to uplift our spirits and
bring us closer to the divine. It is a universal
language that transcends cultural and
linguistic barriers, allowing
us to communicate with the
divine in a way
that words alone
cannot.

"The desire is thy prayers; and if thy desire is without ceasing, thy prayer will also be without ceasing. The continuance of your longing is the continuance of your prayer. "

Saint Augustine

# Crea
# tivity

# Hildegard
## of Bingen

Hildegard of Bingen (c. 1098 – 17 September 1179), also known as Saint Hildegard and the Sibyl of the Rhine, was a German Benedictine abbess and polymath active as a writer, composer, philosopher, mystic, visionary, and as a medical writer and practitioner during the High Middle Ages. She is one of the best known composers of sacred monophony, as well as the most recorded in modern history. She has been considered by scholars to be the founder of scientific natural history in Germany.

From early childhood, long before she undertook her public mission or even her monastic vows, Hildegard's spiritual awareness was grounded in what she called the umbra viventis lucis, the reflection of the living Light. The church remember Hildegard of Bingen on September 17th.

Hildegard of Bingen was a Renaissance woman ahead of her time. Her multifaceted creativity extended to music, writing, herbalism, and even engineering. Her devotion to her pursuits ran parallel to her faith, with the belief that such skills were God-given and meant to be used for the betterment of society. This profound connection to her creative abilities led her to develop mystical experiences that were grounded in the divine. Her music and writings, particularly her illuminations, were seen as spiritual expressions of her vision of the universe and her understanding of God. Her creativity gave her a unique perspective on spirituality that was both innovative and deeply intuitive.

Abbess

Artist

Author

Composer

Mystic

Pharmacist

Poet

Preacher

Theologian

"Like billowing clouds, Like the incessant gurgle of the brook, The longing of the spirit can never be stilled."

— Hildegard von Bingen

The arts are an essential part of our lives, not only for their ability to provide entertainment, but also to evoke emotions and feelings within us that may have been dormant. Art can also be used to express spiritual beliefs and ignite a connection to the divine. All forms of art from performing (music, theater, film, dance) to visual (painting, sculpture, architecture, graphics, design), and even literary (fiction, nonfiction, poetry, playwriting) can help us unlock the power of spiritual exploration.

The arts can be used as vehicles of prayer. As we explore a work of art, we can ask ourselves how it makes us feel emotionally and spiritually. We can also think about the relationship between God and humanity that is expressed in the piece, just like when we look into the Bible for answers. Pause to reflect on any insights you may have. Prayer can also be found through the act of creating art. Being creative mimics the Creator; making art is a way for us to communicate with God that often goes deeper than speaking aloud our prayers.

It's not necessary to be "artistically talented" in order to create art. Everyone has an inner artist within them. Consider praying through painting, sculpting, singing from a hymnal, writing poetry or stories, or even dancing. Art making is a form of prayer itself.

These four pictures were created by asking Artificial Intelligence software to make images of a group of monks praying.

# Reflection

Was the process of creating this work prayerful?

Does the content of a piece of art make a difference to whether you interact with it prayerfully?

Do the images lead you into prayer or meditation?

What do the images say about your own spirituality?

Would Hildegard of Bingen have engaged with Artificial Intelligence as a form of creativity?

# Ecology

# Francis

## of Assisi

Francis of Assisi (1181/1182 – 3 October 1226) was an Italian Catholic friar, deacon and preacher. He founded the men's Order of Friars Minor, the women's Order of Saint Clare, the Third Order of Saint Francis and the Custody of the Holy Land. Francis preached the Christian doctrine that the world was created good and beautiful by God but suffers a need for redemption because of human sin. He believed that all creatures should praise God (a common theme in the Psalms) and the people have a duty to protect and enjoy nature as both the stewards of God's creation and as creatures ourselves. Many of the stories that surround the life of Saint Francis say that he had a great love for animals and the environment. An incident illustrating the Saint's humility towards nature is recounted in the *Little Flowers*, a collection of legends and folklore that sprang up after the Saint's death. One day, while Francis was traveling with some companions, they happened upon a place in the road where birds filled the trees on either side. Francis told his companions to "wait for me while I go to preach to my sisters the birds." The birds surrounded him, intrigued by the power of his voice, and not one of them flew away. He is often portrayed with a bird, typically in his hand.

# Canticle Of The Creatures

Most High, all-powerful, good Lord,
Yours are the praises, the glory, and the honour, and all blessing.

To You alone, Most High, do they belong,
and no human is worthy to mention Your name.

Praised be You, my Lord, with all Your creatures,
especially Sir Brother Sun,
Who is the day and through whom You give us light.

And he is beautiful and radiant with great splendour;
and bears a likeness of You, Most High One.

Praised be You, my Lord, through Sister Moon and the stars,
in heaven You formed them clear and precious and beautiful.

Praised be You, my Lord, through Brother Wind,
and through the air, cloudy and serene, and every kind of weather,
through whom You give sustenance to Your creatures.

Praised be You, my Lord, through Sister Water,
who is very useful and humble and precious and chaste.

Praised be You, my Lord, through Brother Fire,
through whom You light the night,
and he is beautiful and playful and robust and strong.

Praised be You, my Lord, through our Sister Mother Earth,
who sustains and governs us,
and who produces various fruit with coloured flowers and herbs.

Praised be You, my Lord, through those who give pardon for Your
love, and bear infirmity and tribulation.

Blessed are those who endure in peace
for by You, Most High, shall they be crowned.

Praised be You, my Lord, through our Sister Bodily Death,
from whom no one living can escape.

Woe to those who die in mortal sin.
Blessed are those whom death will find in Your most holy will,
for the second death shall do them no harm.

Praise and bless my Lord and give Him thanks
and serve Him with great humility.

Written by St. Francis of Assisi

St. Francis of Assisi, known for his devotion to the natural world, believed that all creatures were interconnected and valued in the eyes of God. He saw the environment as a reflection of God's goodness, deserving of respect and care. To him, prayer was an act of communicating with all of God's creation, including the animals and plants. His spirituality, rooted in the Franciscan tradition, emphasised simplicity and humility, recognising that humans were only a small part of the larger ecosystem. As the seasons changed, St. Francis found meaning in each one, seeing the beauty and wonder in God's creation during every time of the year. St. Francis' love for animals was particularly noteworthy, as he saw them as fellow creatures with whom humans shared the planet. He even preached to birds, believing that they too could hear the word of God. This deep respect for nature and all its inhabitants is a hallmark of Franciscanism, and has continued to influence the way many people view ecology and the environment to this day.

"At all times and seasons, in every country and place, every day and all day, we must have a true and humble faith."

— *Saint Francis*

**Genesis 1:9-10:** Then God said, "Let the waters below the heavens be gathered into one place, and let the dry land appear"; and it was so. God called the dry land earth, and the gathering of the waters He called seas, and God saw that it was good.

**Amos 5:8:** He who made the Pleiades and Orion and changes deep darkness into morning, who also darkens day into night, who calls for the waters of the sea and pours them out on the surface of the earth, the Lord is His name.

**Psalm 104:14:** He causes the grass to grow for the cattle, and herb for the service of man: that he may bring forth food out of the earth.

**Luke 12:27:** Consider the lilies, how they grow: they neither toil nor spin; but I tell you, not even Solomon in all his glory clothed himself like one of these.

**Psalm 96:12:** Let the field be joyful, and all that is therein: then shall all the trees of the wood rejoice.

# Journey Prayer Sticks

Journey sticks are a way for travellers to capture the memories of their journey and share them with others. The concept is simple; you pick up natural items on your travels and attach them to a stick. It can be an effective way to increase our awareness of nature, inspire curiosity, and help us foster a connection with the environment.

You just need a stick, some double-sided tape or rubber bands, and you're ready to hunt for treasures. Each time you find something special, think about where it came from - perhaps a seed that will grow into a tree, leaves that could provide shelter for animals, feathers from beautiful birds, colourful flower petals or grasses - and take the opportunity to express thanks to God for our wonderful world.

At the end of your journey, take the stick back home and look at all the different items you've discovered.

# Solit
# ude

# Julian

## of Norwich

Julian of Norwich (late 1342 – after 1416) was an English anchorite of the Middle Ages. She wrote the earliest surviving book in the English language to be written by a woman, *Revelations of Divine Love*. She lived throughout her life in the English city of Norwich, an important center for commerce that also had a vibrant religious life. In 1373, aged thirty and so seriously ill she thought she was on her deathbed, Julian received a series of visions of the Passion of Christ. She recovered from her illness and wrote two versions of her experiences, the earlier one being completed soon after her recovery, and a much longer version, today known as the Long Text, being written many years later. For much of her life, Julian lived in permanent seclusion as an anchoress in her cell, which was attached to St Julian's Church, Norwich. Nothing is known for certain about Julian's actual name, family, or education, or of her life prior to her becoming an anchoress. Preferring to write anonymously, and seeking isolation from the world, she was nevertheless influential in her own lifetime. Julian is today considered to be an important Christian mystic and theologian.

Pray inwardly, even if you do not enjoy it. It does good, though you feel nothing. Yes, even though you think you are doing nothing.

*- Julian of Norwich*

Julian decided to live out her final days in a house beside a parish church. It may sound like a prison, yet she wasn't lacking of any comfort: there was windows, a servant for her daily needs and even a pet cat to keep the mice away. For a woman of the fourteenth century, having a room to herself with peace and quiet provided an opportunity to think, pray, and eventually write.

Though it could have been easy for Julian to reside in solitary confinement, like a desert or forest, her 'cell' was placed in the middle of a frantic port city: noises, scents, and crowds swirled around her home. Word spread that she was praying for the inhabitants of this bustling town, so people would come to seek advice from her or receive words from God. One window faced an outdoor porch where people had access to speak to Julian through a thick curtain. In return, the citizens presented her with food and other gifts.

It might feel natural to assume she was holier-than-thou by correcting everyone who made mistakes; however, Julian's writings showed us she was not like that. Her heart overflowed with love and appreciation for God's compassion towards all.

"Solitude does not necessarily mean living apart from others; rather, it means never living apart from one's self. It is not about the absence of other people, it is about being fully present to ourselves, whether or not we are with others."

*– from "A Hidden Wholeness" by Parker Palmer*

In solitude I find my peace,
A quiet place where worries cease,
The silence soothes my troubled mind,
And all my fears are left behind.

In solitude, I can reflect,
On all the things that I neglect,
My dreams, my hopes, my deepest fears,
Of all my joys and all my tears.

So let me be in solitude,
And I'll emerge, renewed and shrewd,
With a clearer vision, a focused goal,
Ready to play my destined role.

"It is good to be solitary, for solitude is difficult; that something is difficult must be a reason the more for us to do it. "

— Rainer Maria Rilke

# Pilgrimage

# Bona

## of Pisa

St Bona was born in Pisa in 1156. From an early age she experienced visions, particularly of St James. By the age of ten she had decided to dedicate herself to the Augustinian rule and by 14 had set off on her first journey to see her father, who was fighting in the Crusades near Jerusalem. On her way home she was captured by Muslim pirates in the Mediterranean, wounded and imprisoned. Some fellow Pisans rescued her and brought her home. Bona wasn't put off by those experiences. She soon set out again on a thousand mile pilgrimage to Compostella - this time leading a large group of pilgrims under the auspices of the Knights of St James. She was to make the journey a further nine times, travelling mainly on foot. Bona was cheerful and adventurous: 'full of energy, helpful and unselfish, ready to reassure with her smile those who were sick' - according to a contemporary account. She became ill while setting out on her tenth pilgrimage. Bona managed to reach her little room near the church of San Martino, and died on May 29th in 1207, aged 51.

She is a patron saint of travellers, couriers, tour guides, airline staff and pilgrims.

A pilgrimage is a journey, often into an unknown or foreign place, where a person goes in search of new or expanded meaning about their self, others, nature, or a higher good through the experience. It can lead to a personal transformation, after which the pilgrim returns to their daily life.

Pilgrimages are not just about journeying to a location, but about searching for spiritual or moral significance. It is an act that allows one's belief and faith to take center stage. Often, it involves visiting a shrine or place of importance tied to one's beliefs. However, this pilgrimage can also be metaphorical; a journey into someone's own thoughts and convictions. Religions often hold certain places with high regard. They may be the birthplace, death site, or the location where the founder or saint had their spiritual awakening or calling. As people of faith make this journey, they often come across unexpected challenges and learn more about themselves than they had previously thought possible.

# Suggested Pilgrimage Routes

## Abraham's Path (The Middle East)

This epic 1,243-mile route starts in Harran, Turkey, where God is said to have called upon Abraham to 'go forth', and rambles on through Egypt, Palestine, Israel and Jordan.

## Via Francigena (UK, France & Italy)

A 1,200-mile route connecting Canterbury to Rome via France, the Swiss Alps and the Italian Apennines, passing churches and shrines devoted to St Francis.

## Adam's Peak (Sri Lanka)

In Sri Lanka's Central Highlands, this conical, 7,360ft-high peak is home to a footprint that's said to belong to, faith depending, Adam, Buddha or Shiva.

## Caminho Português (Portugal & Spain)

The wild Atlantic coast unravels before you on this uncrowded trail from Lisbon (380 miles) or Porto (140 miles) to Santiago de Compostela.

## Mount Kailash (Tibet)

This three-day, 32-mile circuit of sacred 21,778ft Mount Kailash in Tibet is a holy ritual said to bring good fortune.

## Lourdes (France)

The 92-mile Piemont Route connects St-Jean-Pied-de-Port and Lourdes, a holy pilgrimage site since 1858, when Bernadette Soubirous claimed to have witnessed 18 apparitions of the Virgin Mary.

## St Magnus Way (Scotland)

The wide-open horizons, space and silence of Orkney's coastline enthrall on this 58-mile route honouring the island's patron saint.

## Kumano Kodō (Japan)

This network of ancient trails dives into the remote, densely forested, shrine-topped mountains of the Kii Peninsula, Japan's spiritual heartland.

## Via Coloniensis (Germany)

Grand abbeys and palaces punctuate this 152-mile trail, uniting the former Roman cities of Cologne and Trier, where fourth-century St Peter's Cathedral is a highlight.

## St Finbarr's Way (Ireland)

Traversing three mountain ranges, this 22-mile pilgrimage begins at the Top of the Rock in Dromdaleague, County Cork, where sixth-century monk St Finbarr once preached.

*Published in the May 2021 issue of National Geographic Traveller (UK)*

To go on pilgrimage is not simply to visit a place to admire its treasures of nature, art or history. To go on pilgrimage really means to step out of ourselves in order to encounter God where he has revealed himself, where his grace has shone with particular splendour and produced rich fruits of conversion and holiness among those who believe. Above all, Christians go on pilgrimage to the Holy Land, to the places associated with the Lord's passion, death and resurrection. They go to Rome, the city of the martyrdom of Peter and Paul, and also to Compostela, which, associated with the memory of Saint James, has welcomed pilgrims from throughout the world who desire to strengthen their spirit with the Apostle's witness of faith and love.

- Pope Benedict XVI

**"**

"None of your knowledge, your reading, your connections will be of any use here: two legs suffice, and big eyes to see with. Walk alone, across mountains or through forests. You are nobody to the hills or the thick boughs heavy with greenery. You are no longer a role, or a status, not even an individual, but a body, a body that feels sharp stones on the paths, the caress of long grass and the freshness of the wind. When you walk, the world has neither present nor future: nothing but the cycle of mornings and evenings. Always the same thing to do all day: walk. But the walker who marvels while walking ... has no past, no plans, no experience. He has within him the eternal child. While walking I am but a simple gaze."

- Frédéric Gros

10

# Rhythm

# Peter

## the Apostle

St. Peter the Apostle, originally named Simeon or Simon, was a disciple of Jesus and is recognised as the leader of the 12 disciples by the Roman Catholic Church. He was called to be a follower of Jesus in the early stages of his ministry and given the name Cephas, which when translated into Greek is Petros, also known as Peter. After Jesus ascended to Heaven, Peter was invigorated by the Holy Spirit and taught his fellow disciples how to pray. We see evidence of this from the day of Pentecost onwards, where the apostles kept a rigorous daily prayer routine.

The church remembers Peter the Apostle on June 29th along with St. Paul.

# Liturgy of the Hours

The Liturgy of the Hours, along with the Eucharist, is a prayer practice that has been an integral part of the Church's public worship from the beginning. It is observed by Christians of both Eastern and Western traditions (including Latin Catholic, Eastern Catholic, Eastern Orthodox, Oriental Orthodox, Assyrian, Anglican, Lutheran and some Protestant churches) in various forms and under different names. The custom of praying at specific times of day or night stems back to Jewish traditions; early Christian prayers used elements similar to those used by Jews: chanting psalms, reading Old Testament texts, subsequently adding readings from the Gospels and epistles as well as canticles. Other components were introduced throughout the centuries.

In the Psalms are found expressions like

"in the morning I offer you my prayer"

"At midnight I will rise and thank you"

"Evening, morning and at noon I will cry and lament"

"Seven times a day I praise you"

# Reflection

The Apostles observed the Jewish custom of praying at the third, sixth, and ninth hours, and at midnight. How might your life be transformed if you were to take on this challenge? Even if just a sentence or two of thanks when you woke up, during lunch and as you go to sleep...

# Selah

(ˈsilə ; ˈsiˌlɑ ; sɛˈlɑ ) noun. a Hebrew word at the end of verses in the Psalms:

It's a small word with great meaning. Scholars suggest that this poetic term was peppered throughout the Psalms as a reminder to stop, contemplate, ruminate and praise. It is probably either a liturgical-musical mark or an instruction on the reading of the text, with the meaning of 'stop and listen'. Another proposal is that selah can be used to indicate that there is to be a musical interlude at that point in the Psalm. Greater than a comma, a colon or a full-stop; *Selah* is an invitation. An invitation to having a rhythm in your prayers, in your reading of the psalms, in your meditation and contemplation. Perhaps Selah is a spiritual call to punctuate our daily lives with the divine.

Our Father, who art in heaven,
hallowed be thy name;
thy kingdom come;
thy will be done;
on earth as it is in heaven.
Give us this day our daily bread.
And forgive us our trespasses,
as we forgive those who trespass against us.
And lead us not into temptation;
but deliver us from evil.
For thine is the kingdom,
the power and the glory,
for ever and ever.
Amen.

"May I have the courage today
To live the life that I would love,
To postpone my dream no longer,
But do at last what I came here for
And waste my heart on fear no
more."


— John O'Donohue

The words printed here are concepts. You must go through the experiences.

Saint Augustine